Called:?!

FOLLOWING A FUTURE FILLED WITH THE POSSIBLE

J.D. Walt

SEEDBED PUBLISHING
ASBURY THEOLOGICAL SEMINARY

CALLED:?! FOLLOWING A FUTURE FILLED WITH THE POSSIBLE
Published by Seedbed: Sowing for a Great Awakening
An initiative of Asbury Theological Seminary

©2011 ALL RIGHTS RESERVED
No part of this publication may be reproduced, stored in a retrieval system, or transmitted, in any form or by any means—electronic, mechanical, photocopying, recording, or otherwise—without prior written permission.

To purchase copies of this book, visit asburyseedbed.com.
Design by Stephanie Wright

ISBN: 978-0-914368-00-7

*For my Mom and Dad,
whose lives helped me hear.*

J.D.W.

FOLLOWING A FUTURE FILLED WITH THE POSSIBLE

This little book will help you because we designed it for you. Like so many others, you hold deep within you a sense of purpose for your life, even a sense of destiny. Something tucked away in the recesses of your soul will not be quiet. Even the whisper of this voice reminds you that your life was meant for "something more."

You are called.

I remember wrestling with this as a law student. My career plans were unfolding nicely. My resume shined with promise. All seemed right on track, but something told me I was on the wrong track. A new song stirred in my heart and I had no idea what to do with it.

I made an appointment with the pastor of the church I attended. After listening to me talk for five or six minutes, a look came over his face—one that said, "I know exactly what you need." He made a beeline for the bookshelf where he pulled a gigantic three-ring binder and set it in my lap. OMG! I thought. He told me I would need to enter into a process where I would be assigned a "mentor" (that would not be him) who would supervise me as I answered all the questions in this "gauntlet" of a manual. After that would come a two or three year process of waiting, which would likely involve a graduate degree in theological education.

I left his office scratching my head. He validated the sense of calling happening within me. But he wrongly assumed this necessarily meant I wanted to do what he was doing. Because of my strong spiritual pulse, I guess he assumed I was called to be an ordained minister.

In retrospect, I guess he was right. Today I serve as an ordained minister. His approach to me, however, was all wrong. I needed my pastor to be a mentor. He gave me a manual that came with an institutional supervisor.

Somewhere in the ensuing season I met a campus minister who invited me into a journey which looked a lot more like the landscape of this little book. He knew I wasn't searching for a career path. He understood I was responding to something much deeper. He helped me take those first steps into a "called" life.

A "called" life means many things for many people. It can literally take the form of any job under the sun. It might mean serving as the pastor of a church. It might mean serving as a member of congress. To embrace the "called" life does not narrow the scope of the future. It opens up the horizon.

Stephen Johnson, an author and thinker, researches and writes about where ideas come from. He coined the term, "the adjacent possible." Here's how he describes it:

> *The adjacent possible is a kind of shadow future, hovering on the edges of the present state of things, a map of all the ways in which the present can reinvent itself.*

The 21 day journey ahead invites you to walk on the pathway that leads to the "adjacent possible." As you already know, this journey looks more like Jacob wrestling than career counseling. It's more about finding a posture from which to behold the future, rather than a place to brainstorm on a whiteboard. **The "called" life chiefly involves learning to behold God—Jesus Christ—In such fashion that you become his protégé in the making.**

In the final analysis, the adjacent possible is the Kingdom of God—the future of the possible. It hovers on the edges of the present state of things. Those who embrace this life become demonstration plots of the adjacent possible, "on Earth as it is in Heaven," in the real world.

Called:
From Darkness to Light

In the beginning God created the heavens and the earth. Now the earth was formless and empty, darkness was over the surface of the deep, and the Spirit of God was hovering over the waters. And God said, "Let there be light," and there was light. GENESIS 1:1-3

And so it began. The story of Creation and the plot of Redemption masterfully narrate us into the epic movement from darkness to light.

The bedtime rituals at our home, on good nights, close out with exuberant, raucous worship. One memory stands out from a few years back. We were singing and dancing to my friend David Crowder's rendition of *I Saw the Light*. You recognize it as the work of the late great gospel theologian, Hank Williams Sr.

> *I saw the Light. I saw the Light.*
> *No more darkness. No more night.*
> *Now I'm so happy, no trouble in sight.*
> *Praise the Lord! I saw the Light!*

Can you see it? *I Saw the Light* blaring, the Lord Jesus Christ shining and five of us jubilantly dancing. (This was the BS period—before our son Sam—we had a 5 year old, 3 year old and 20 month old.) In the midst of that irrational exuberance I began to point to a large painting of Jesus on the wall.

You see, I'm trying to teach my children to worship, but in the moment about to unfold, everything would change. I became the student, and my children the teachers. David (5) danced over to the table and picked up an empty communion chalice. He got my attention as he lifted it over his head, turned it upside down and began to dance with unbridled joy. Mary Kathryn (3) not to be outdone ran over to the window and grabbed a wooden cross she and David hammered together, lifting it into the air over her head and continued her dance. Now Lily (20 months) who will not be outdone, runs over to the massive painting of Jesus crucified and rockets both of her hands upward as though to signal a touchdown and she just stood there still, seemingly mesmerized by what was happening.

It gets better. Mary Kathryn put the cross down and picked up the world, lifting the small globe from the table and over her head in triumphal dance. And there I am, thunderstruck, tears streaming down my face, all the images and ideas racing through my mind.

I saw the Light that night; pure illumination. And in the brightness I understood my calling in the simplest and profoundest terms: to Shine.

The light shines in the darkness, and the darkness has not overcome it. JOHN 1:5

For God, who said, "Let light shine out of darkness," made his light shine in our hearts to give us the light of the knowledge of the glory of God in the face of Christ. 2 CORINTHIANS 4:6

JOURNAL

Have you seen the Light? Can you tell your own story in the framework of the movement from darkness to Light? Sketch out the movements the way a movie maker would caption the tracks on a DVD. Or you might try making two columns, one for "darkness" and the other "Light." Now capture particular transformations in your own life through these contrasts.

Called:
From Death to Life

Then Jesus came from Galilee to the Jordan to be baptized by John. But John tried to deter him, saying, "I need to be baptized by you, and do you come to me?"

Jesus replied, "Let it be so now; it is proper for us to do this to fulfill all righteousness." Then John consented.

As soon as Jesus was baptized, he went up out of the water. At that moment heaven was opened, and he saw the Spirit of God descending like a dove and lighting on him. And a voice from heaven said, "This is my Son, whom I love; with him I am well pleased."

MATTHEW 3:13-17

It's a fascinating mark of calling. In the water that day, the second person of the Trinity heard the adoring voice of the first person of the Trinity, while being embraced by the third person of the Trinity. Ever since, every person who ever lived is invited into this Divine community through this ordinary water. The Spirit hovers over the waters ready to embrace. The Father speaks words of a gifted identity. The baptized becomes clothed in Christ. New Creation springs forth. The old life of sin and death is buried in the grave. The Risen Life of Christ literally springs forth in us.

This most fundamental calling echoes through the rest of the New Testament.

To the Romans:

Or don't you know that all of us who were baptized into Christ Jesus were baptized into his death? We were therefore buried with him through baptism into death in order that, just as Christ was raised from the dead through the glory of the Father, we too may live a new life. ROMANS 6:3-4

To the Galatians:

I have been crucified with Christ and I no longer live, but Christ lives in me. The life I live in the body, I live by faith in the Son of God, who loved me and gave himself for me. GALATIANS 2:20

To the Ephesians:

But because of his great love for us, God, who is rich in mercy, made us alive with Christ even when we were dead in transgressions—it is by grace you have been saved. EPHESIANS 2:4-5

To the Colossians:

For you died, and your life is now hidden with Christ in God. When Christ, who is your life, appears, then you also will appear with him in glory. COLOSSIANS 3:3-4

Because of the presence of Jesus Christ, ordinary waters become living water. To be baptized in the Triune name means to literally stand "in Christ," buried with him in his death and raised with him in his life. **The old life is "drowned." The new life is risen.**

Here's the best part. Those words the Father spoke over Jesus in the power of the Spirit, he speaks over you personally.

(Insert your name) you are my son/daughter. You are my beloved. With you, I am well pleased. The quest for "self-realization" ends. The pilgrimage of "call actualization" begins.

JOURNAL

Write that last sentence inserting your name in your own handwriting. Speak it aloud over yourself repeatedly for the next 20 days as you begin the day's reading. Allow these words to pass through your ears to be "heard" in your deepest heart. Meditate, ponder and sit in awe of the reality of your own baptism. Draw your deepest identity from those waters. This is where the Gospel begins. To repent means simply to renounce and turn away from the lies spoken over you and to embrace the truth God speaks over you. Ask the Spirit to reveal what those lies may be and write them down. In time, they will be drowned in death.

3 Called:
To a Life of Extraordinary Epiphany

Then Jesus was led by the Spirit into the desert to be tempted by the devil. After fasting forty days and forty nights, he was hungry. The tempter came to him and said, "If you are the Son of God, tell these stones to become bread."

Jesus answered, "It is written: 'Man does not live on bread alone, but on every word that comes from the mouth of God.'" MATTHEW 4:1-4

From the mountain top experience of baptism, the Spirit leads Jesus into the arid valley of the desert. Calling works this way. Word and Spirit must do their refining work within us. As the songwriter David Baroni wrote:

> Lord You took me out of Egypt
> Now take Egypt out of me
> You delivered me from Pharaoh now set me free from me
> Let my heart become a promised land
> Where the desert used to be
> Lord You took me out of Egypt
> Now take Egypt out of me.

Note how the temptations attempt to get Jesus to disavow his God-given identity and validate himself. "If you are the Son of God, tell these stones to become bread."

Some years back I sat in a weekly Bible study with a group of students. We focused on fasting together and feasting on God's Word together through the 40 days of Lent. One day one of the students shared a powerful epiphany he had about Jesus' response to the first temptation concerning living on every word that comes from the mouth of God. Here's what he said:

"I think the word Jesus was living on in the desert was the word that had just literally come from the mouth of God at his baptism: 'This is my Son, my beloved; with him I am well pleased.'"

This thought made perfect sense though it never occurred to me before. Jesus fasted from food such that this baptismal blessing word could nourish him in the deepest place.

This is our calling—to eat this Word, until it literally becomes our identity, the shape of our deepest self.

It gets better. When the Word of God becomes for us the Bread of Life, our lives become that bread in the hands of Christ, broken, multiplied and given for others. Vocation comes from the Latin word, vocare meaning, "voice." This Voice of our Father creates us anew by the gift of this baptismal word of blessing. He gives us an identity rooted in the life of his Son. It doesn't stop there, though. As this Divine Voice resonates in our mind and heart, it begins to shape our vocation—the way the Voice of God gets expressed through our lives into the every day World. In this way, what we do springs from who we are rather than the more common scenario of an identity built around our performance.

It all comes full circle at the Lord's Table, in the Bread and Wine. We pray, "Pour out your Spirit on us gathered here and on these gifts of bread and wine. Make them be for us the Body and Blood of Christ *so that we may be for the world the Body of Christ redeemed by his blood.*"

"Do this," he said, "in remembrance of me."

JOURNAL

Examine your life to date and consider how you might have based your sense of self and identity on your job or your performance in some fashion. As you continue to feast on the baptismal, blessing words of God over your life, consider how this kind of blessing flows through your life to others. Where do you experience the joy of your life becoming bread for others?

4 Called:
From Ladder Climbing to Cross Descending

Have the same mind in you that was in Christ Jesus, who, being in very nature God, did not consider equality with God something to be grasped, but made himself nothing, taking the very nature of a servant, being made in human likeness. And being found in appearance as a man, he humbled himself and became obedient to death— even death on a cross! Therefore God exalted him to the highest place and gave him the name that is above every name, that at the name of Jesus every knee should bow, in heaven and on earth and under the earth, and every tongue confess that Jesus Christ is Lord, to the glory of God the Father. PHILIPPIANS 2:5-11

Perhaps the biggest temptation we face in life is that of becoming someone other than who God made us to be. That's what happened in the Garden. The tempter framed the opportunity as one of becoming like or equal with God, as though the call to bear God's image wasn't enough.

Note how the one "who being in very nature God, did not consider equality with God something to be grasped, but made himself nothing."

This climbing quest continued as the broken image bearers ascended all the way to the heavens as they built the high tower of Babel, to "make a name for themselves."

Note how Jesus "humbled himself and became obedient to death—even death on a cross!" He descended.

Consider how the ones who sought to "make a name for themselves" watched all of their efforts come to nothing. They fell from their exalted place and to this day their name is "mud."

Now look at how the one who "made himself nothing" is "exalted to the highest place and given the name that is above every name."

It's fascinating how God ceased the construction project, confused their language and scattered them to the four corners of the Earth. Now note how it all ultimately comes back together: "Every knee should bow… and every tongue confess that Jesus Christ is Lord, to the glory of God the Father." The Cross actually confuses the confusion and brings forth the very song of Heaven.

Our calling could not be more clear. We are "to have this same mind in us." The best part: This mind is given to us as we give ourselves to Jesus. This pathway of descent cannot be found in a particular place or job. It's possibility is in every place and job.

Many recount the story of Mother Teresa's encounter with a young man who had come from North America to work in her mission. They assigned him a desk job requiring a lot of paper work. He complained to Mother, "I'm not called or gifted for administrative work. My vocation is to serve the poor." She wryly responded, *"No son, your vocation is not to serve the poor. Your vocation is to belong to Jesus."*

JOURNAL

Invite the Holy Spirit to search your mind and to ferret out the ways in which the ancient mind of Adam still holds sway. Do you need to be recognized for your accomplishments? Where in the building project of your life do you secretly (or openly) try to "make a name for yourself?" Where does this need to be famous come from? Now run back to the waters of baptism and the Word of the Father over you. Find ways to starve those competing ambitions to become someone "important." What are those secret ways you might "belong to Jesus" today?

 Called:
From "How much do I give?" to "How much do I keep?"

Six days before the Passover, Jesus arrived at Bethany, where Lazarus lived, whom Jesus had raised from the dead. Here a dinner was given in Jesus' honor. Martha served, while Lazarus was among those reclining at the table with him. Then Mary took about a pint of pure nard, an expensive perfume; she poured it on Jesus' feet and wiped his feet with her hair. And the house was filled with the fragrance of the perfume.

JOHN 12:1-3

Can you smell it? The fragrance of the perfume still lingers in the air. Every year, if not every day, since this happened over 2000 years ago, this story is told, remembered and reveled in. In another Gospel account, when a similar, if not the same story, is told, Jesus responds to his scorning disciples saying,

I tell you the truth, wherever this gospel is preached throughout the world, what she has done will also be told, in memory of her.

MATTHEW 26:13

I define an ordinary saint as a person whose life cannot be discussed without also talking about the life of Jesus. A saint is one whose life makes no sense apart from God. When a person gets lost in the worship of this God, their life becomes lost in his service. **The life of one who answers the call to worship the risen Son of God becomes something of an "outlier" in the world. Sadly, all too often, they become something of an anomaly in the Church.** Some admire them without understanding them and say things like, "I really admire what you are doing." Under their breath they whisper, "Better you than me." Others quietly talk about the "waste" of their life.

All the while, the one pouring out the perfume searches for a song such as, "Were the whole realm of nature mine, that were an offering far too small. Love so amazing so Divine, demands my soul, my life my all."[1]

Regardless of role or job description, lay or clergy, paid or not, this story captures the most essential calling of our lives—the call to worship. I'm not talking about worship as "singing," but worship as a life lost in the Song. Clearly, this woman got carried away in her worship. It made everyone around uncomfortable. It always does.

Garrison Keillor, in one of his distinctive radio broadcasts, described a Thanksgiving experience in Minnesota. Keillor said that his extended family gathered around a long dinner table that almost creaked under the weight of a turkey-centered feast.

"Then," said Keillor, "the hostess made the mistake of calling on Uncle John to pray. Everybody in the family knew that Uncle John couldn't pray without talking about the cross and crying. And if there is one thing that makes people nervous, it's listening to a grown man cry. Sure enough, Uncle John prayed, talked about the cross, and cried. Meanwhile, the rest of us shifted nervously from one foot to the other and longed for the prayer to end."

Keillor then inserted this powerful observation: "All of us knew that Jesus died on the cross for us, but Uncle John had never gotten over it."

JOURNAL

Dwell on the image of the woman pouring out the perfume on Jesus' feet. Describe what must be going on in her mind and heart. As you look around the room, pick a few other people and journal what might be going on in their inner response to this scene. Sketch out the different ways you see yourself in this scene.

---

[1] Issac Watts, "When I survey the Wondrous Cross," 1707.

6 Called: From Dutiful Discipline to an "Abiding Desire"

"I am the true vine, and my Father is the Farmer. He cuts off every branch in me that bears no fruit, while every branch that does bear fruit he prunes so that it will be even more fruitful. You are already clean because of the word I have spoken to you. Abide in me, as I also abide in you. No branch can bear fruit by itself; it must abide in the vine. Neither can you bear fruit unless you abide in me.

"I am the vine; you are the branches. If you abide in me and I in you, you will bear much fruit; apart from me you can do nothing. If you do not abide in me, you are like a branch that is thrown away and withers; such branches are picked up, thrown into the fire and burned. If you abide in me and my words abide in you, ask whatever you wish, and it will be done for you. This is to my Father's glory, that you bear much fruit, showing yourselves to be my disciples. JOHN 15:1-8

Dedication to devotion is not the goal. Discipline in spiritual practices is not the goal. Abiding does not consist in ratcheting up your "quiet time" a few notches. So what, you ask, is the goal? The goal is the life hid with Christ in God. If the secret to abiding is not dedication or devotion or discipline, then what is it?

Desire.

"One thing I ask of the Lord," says the Psalmist, "this only do I seek: that I may dwell in the house of the Lord all the days of my life, to gaze on the beauty of the Lord and to seek him in his temple." PSALM 27:4

Danish theologian, Soren Kierkegaard, famously said, "Purity of heart is to will one thing."

Our desires determine both our direction and destination. Yet so much devotional energy gets spent fighting against desire. Certainly, the desires seated deeply within our broken human nature lead us in the wrong direction. Freedom from these broken desires comes not from striving to overcome them via our devotional habits. Doing so can lead to a place where our habits stand in the way of our holiness. We become devoted to our devotion. One may look the part on the outside, while inside the war rages.

We need a reorientation of desire that comes from a total renovation of the heart. This is why Jesus doesn't spend his time developing strategies of sin management. The repentance he calls for and empowers cuts to the core of our desires and reorients them in such a way that they can be trusted instead of resisted. This is the liberty of the sons and daughters of God. This is what pruning and abiding are all about.

To move forward in response to the call of God might mean trading in the consistency of your devotion for the constancy of his abiding. It might seem a subtle distinction. In the end, it will make all the difference. To be sure, discipline is a step in the right direction—remember discipline is not the goal.

JOURNAL

How much time do you spend on a daily basis fighting your desires? How do your desires compete with one another and create internal conflict? How do you understand and interpret what this idea might mean to your "devotional" life? Allow yourself to wrestle with the challenge it may present.

Called:
From "Saving the World" to "Serving my Friends"

It was just before the Passover Feast. Jesus knew that the time had come for him to leave this world and go to the Father. Having loved his own who were in the world, he now showed them the full extent of his love. The evening meal was being served, and the devil had already prompted Judas Iscariot, son of Simon, to betray Jesus. Jesus knew that the Father had put all things under his power, and that he had come from God and was returning to God; so he got up from the meal, took off his outer clothing, and wrapped a towel around his waist. After that, he poured water into a basin and began to wash his disciples' feet, drying them with the towel that was wrapped around him.

JOHN 13:1-5

When one gets a sense that they are being called by God their immediate response often leads them to look for some way to get more involved in "church." It's a good impulse, but it can lead to an adventure in missing the point. We all too quickly translate our "calling" into some urgent method or program to "save the world."

All the while, this calling boils down to one word—"Love." God doesn't save the world through a few hyper-zealous, religious busybodies. God saves the world through small communities of people who "love one another" to an extraordinary degree.

In this scene, we see Jesus performing the most menial task with the most exquisite care. The washing of feet happened daily. It had to be done. Someone always had to do it. This was a nondescript practice that went without note. Except this time the gospel writer took copious notes. John could have taken four words, "Jesus washed their feet," to describe what happened. Instead, he took 132. Watch this:

1. He got up from the table
2. He took off his outer garment
3. He wrapped himself in a towel.
4. He began to wash his disciples feet,
5. drying them with the towel with which he was girded.

"So," you say, "he washed their feet." "No," John says. "He showed them the full extent of his love." Not even the greatest artists in history see this reality. Do a Google image search on "Jesus washes his disciples feet," and see what's wrong with most all of the paintings. Look carefully.

Now that I, your Lord and Teacher, have washed your feet, you also should wash one another's feet (v.14).

If our "calling" does not express itself in extravagant love to those closest to us, we may well be off the trail. To be clear, Jesus calls us to serve the world around us in every way, shape and form; yet, he approaches it differently. The most significant service we can offer the world, he seems to say, happens in the way we serve each other. Our connection to him manifests itself in responding to the calling to love one another. Two chapters later, in the midst of a teaching on "fruit-bearing," he makes plain the secret:

"Greater love has no one than this, to lay down their life for their friends." JOHN 15:13

JOURNAL

Draw three concentric circles on the page. In the innermost circle write the names of your immediate family. In the next ring outward, write the names of several Christian friends. Be sure to include at least one EGR (Extra Grace Required) in there. In the outermost circle, write the names of persons in your life who do not follow Jesus. Jot down ways you might fill those innermost circles with the variety of love we see in Jesus. Consider how the love in the inner circles impact the outer circle.

Called:
From a Predictable Life to "Leaving the Building"

The Lord had said to Abram, "Leave your native country, your relatives, and your father's family, and go to the land that I will show you. I will make you into a great nation. I will bless you and make you famous, and you will be a blessing to others. I will bless those who bless you and curse those who treat you with contempt. All the families on earth will be blessed through you." So Abram departed as the Lord had instructed, and Lot went with him. Abram was seventy-five years old when he left Haran. He took his wife, Sarai, his nephew Lot, and all his wealth—his livestock and all the people he had taken into his household at Haran—and headed for the land of Canaan. When they arrived in Canaan, Abram traveled through the land as far as Shechem. There he set up camp beside the oak of Moreh. At that time, the area was inhabited by Canaanites. GENESIS 12:1-6

It's one thing to leave; it's quite another not to know where you are going. Who does this? More often than not, the call of God works this way. This story is not about destination or even vocation. This text comes down to three realities: Abraham (Sarah), God and faith.

By faith Abraham, when called to go to a place he would later receive as his inheritance, obeyed and went, even though he did not know where he was going. By faith he made his home in the promised land like a stranger in a foreign country; he lived in tents, as did Isaac and Jacob, who were heirs with him of the same promise. For he was looking forward to the city with foundations, whose architect and builder is God. HEBREWS 11:8B-10

To be called by God is not so much about going to do a particular job in a particular place. Answering the call means abandoning yourself to God. Calling often means a catastrophic upsetting of the apple cart, a complete change in ambition, a reorientation of direction, a defining exercise of faith, leading one across a threshold into a whole new land of possibility.

Two little words capture the whole movement: "Abram left."

Chances are if you are reading this short "field guide," you've already left the building. It might not have involved a U-Haul, but you left the building project known as your life. You may still live in your old home, but your heart now lives in the "Tent of Meeting." You may still be doing your old job, but your mind races with ambition for the new thing the Holy Spirit is up to in the world.

Before we go further, let's get one thing settled. **Our first, middle and last calling is not to a place or a position or a role. It is to a person, the person of Jesus Christ.**

Two little words capture the whole movement: "Follow me."

The celebrated Trappist Monk, Thomas Merton, penned these words as a prayer in one of his journals along the way. They've captured the praying heart of the "called" for decades since.

> *MY LORD GOD, I have no idea where I am going. I do not see the road ahead of me. I cannot know for certain where it will end. Nor do I really know myself, and the fact that I think I am following your will does not mean that I am actually doing so. But I believe that the desire to please you does in fact please you. And I hope I have that desire in all that I am doing. I hope that I will never do anything apart from that desire. And I know that if I do this, you will lead me by the right road, though I may know nothing about it. Therefore, I will trust you always, though I may seem to be lost and in the shadow of death. I will not fear, for you are ever with me, and you will never leave me to face my perils alone.*[2]

---

2   Thomas Merton, *Thoughts in Solitude*.

JOURNAL

Spend five minutes praying through this prayer. Now try crafting this kind of prayer from your own words. Work at capturing the honesty of your present condition. Write your prayer below.

 Called:
To a Continuous Process Filled with Moments of Crisis

Then the Lord appeared to Abram and said, "I will give this land to your descendants." And Abram built an altar there and dedicated it to the Lord, who had appeared to him. After that, Abram traveled south and set up camp in the hill country, with Bethel to the west and Ai to the east. There he built another altar and dedicated it to the Lord, and he worshiped the Lord. Then Abram continued traveling south by stages toward the Negev. GENESIS 12:7-9

The call of God comes by crisis and through process. Abram travels "by stages;" yet, he builds altars. He readies himself for ever-unfolding Revelation. Note the ancient pattern: God reveals. Abram responds. Watch how he does it. In the short span of two verses Abram builds two altars. He makes visible representations of invisible realities.

Listening for and responding to the voice of God can get confusing. What seemed so clear months ago can be easily doubted today. One asks, "Was that God or was that me? Did I hear right?" The tendency to rationalize and reinterpret tempts us all. Moments must be marked. It's not so important to journal every thought process and feeling along the way. It is essential to capture the major moments. This calling can only be sorted out by walking in the way of stone-stacking, altar-building worship, and more often than not, we are only shown the next step.

Soren Kierkegaard once said something to this effect, "Life must be lived forwards, but it can only be understood backwards." Capturing crucial moments empowers the process of remembrance that unfolds the pathway of discernment.

This will not only help you process the calling of God, but it will leave a trail of wisdom for others to follow as they do the same. Where would we be without the altars of those who have gone before us?

The movement-launching event we know as "Aldersgate" continues to guide millions because John Wesley captured the moment with paper and ink. The 34-year-old Anglican Priest took 88 words and formed them into an altar of remembrance that continues to fan the flames of worship to this very day.

> *In the evening I went very unwillingly to a society in Aldersgate Street, where one was reading Luther's preface to the Epistle to the Romans. About a quarter before nine, while the leader was describing the change which God works in the heart through faith in Christ, I felt my heart strangely warmed. I felt I did trust in Christ alone for salvation; and an assurance was given me that He had taken away my sins, even mine, and saved me from the law of sin and death.*[3]

JOURNAL

Do you have an "Aldersgate" like story in your life? Can you remember a particularly strong "break-through" of the grace of God? Try storyboarding it somewhere on this page.

---

[3] *The Journal of John Wesley.* May 24, 1738.

10 Called:
To Believe the Impossible

> When Abram was ninety-nine years old, the LORD appeared to him and said, "I am God Almighty; walk before me faithfully and be blameless. Then I will make my covenant between me and you and will greatly increase your numbers." Abram fell facedown, and God said to him, "As for me, this is my covenant with you: You will be the father of many nations. No longer will you be called Abram; your name will be Abraham, for I have made you a father of many nations. I will make you very fruitful; I will make nations of you, and kings will come from you. I will establish my covenant as an everlasting covenant between me and you and your descendants after you for the generations to come, to be your God and the God of your descendants after you. The whole land of Canaan, where you now reside as a foreigner, I will give as an everlasting possession to you and your descendants after you; and I will be their God." GENESIS 17:1-8

If, for some reason, you thought you were too old to say "yes" to God's calling on your life, think again. At 99 Abram is just getting started. The revelation of God progresses as Abram processes. By now God made several massive promises despite Abram's several epic fails. Note how exalted Divinity chooses to work with fallen humanity. It's a major theme of calling. God relentlessly pursues those he calls. And the God who calls makes audacious promises. God promises to make a 99-year-old, childless man the father of many nations. God promises to give a man living in a tent in a foreign land the whole country. God enters into a covenant with Abram, and as a sign of it, God changes Abram's name to Abraham.

This is not some kind of vocational transaction or job description or to-do list. In fact, God promises to do the whole thing. "I have made… I will make… I will make… I will establish… I will give… I will be." God doesn't give Abraham a job. He tells him who he is. The only thing remotely resembling a job are these three words, "You will be."

The calling of God is about an identity long before it becomes a vocation. The truth? Until we accept the gift of our identity from the God who made us, we will burn ourselves out working to prove we are actually somebody. In the words of the Babylonian tower builders, "Let us make a name for ourselves."

Burnout doesn't come from working too hard. It comes from not knowing who you are.

John Wesley captured this critical idea of identity before vocation in his celebrated prayer below. He locates his work in ministry between these identifiers, "I am thine and thou art mine."

> *I am no longer my own, but thine.*
> *Put me to what thou wilt, rank me with whom thou wilt.*
> *Put me to doing, put me to suffering.*
> *Let me be employed for thee or laid aside for thee,*
> *exalted for thee or brought low for thee.*
> *Let me be full, let me be empty.*
> *Let me have all things, let me have nothing.*
> *I freely and heartily yield all things to thy pleasure and disposal.*
> *And now, O glorious and blessed God, Father, Son and Holy Spirit,*
> *thou art mine, and I am thine.*
> *So be it.*
> *And the covenant which I have made on earth,*
> *let it be ratified in heaven.*
> *Amen.*[4]

---

4   *Book of Offices of the British Methodist Church*, "John Wesley's Covenant Prayer" 1936.

JOURNAL

Which of the lines in this covenant prayer are most difficult for you to pray? Where are the rubs? Wrestle with these words in prayer. Memorize them so you can work with them in your spirit at all times. This is indeed one of the great practices of the "called."

11 Called:
From Self-Assuredness to God-Confidence

Now Moses was tending the flock of Jethro his father-in-law, the priest of Midian, and he led the flock to the far side of the wilderness and came to Horeb, the mountain of God. There the angel of the LORD appeared to him in flames of fire from within a bush. Moses saw that though the bush was on fire it did not burn up. So Moses thought, "I will go over and see this strange sight—why the bush does not burn up." When the LORD saw that he had gone over to look, God called to him from within the bush, "Moses! Moses!" And Moses said, "Here I am." "Do not come any closer," God said. "Take off your sandals, for the place where you are standing is holy ground."

Then he said, "I am the God of your father, the God of Abraham, the God of Isaac and the God of Jacob." At this, Moses hid his face, because he was afraid to look at God. The LORD said, "I have indeed seen the misery of my people in Egypt. I have heard them crying out because of their slave drivers, and I am concerned about their suffering. So I have come down to rescue them from the hand of the Egyptians and to bring them up out of that land into a good and spacious land, a land flowing with milk and honey—the home of the Canaanites, Hittites, Amorites, Perizzites, Hivites and Jebusites. And now the cry of the Israelites has reached me, and I have seen the way the Egyptians are oppressing them.

So now, go. I am sending you to Pharaoh to bring my people the Israelites out of Egypt." But Moses said to God, "Who am I that I should go to Pharaoh and bring the Israelites out of Egypt?" And God said, "I will be with you. And this will be the sign to you that it is I who have sent you: When you have brought the people out of Egypt, you will worship God on this mountain." EXODUS 3:1-12

Moses was a child of Israel who survived the slaughter, a son of Pharaoh who enjoyed palatial privileges, and a servant of Jethro herding sheep on the backside of nowhere. One of these things is not like the other. Moses would spend the first half of his life wandering in the wilderness of exile and the latter half wandering in the wilderness of return. His life bore all the marks of being set apart for something big, yet his call came pretty late in the game. Did he need to be stripped of some self-perceived importance? Did he need to take a prerequisite course before he could hear the call, perhaps a course in weakness awareness?

From an ark made of reeds to a bush bathed in fire, God called a delivered one to take on the role of a deliverer. These wilderness years brought his strong self-assuredness to nothing. Once a violent young man filled with vindictiveness, Moses now stammered in meekness.

In following the call of God, our natural strengths and abilities must often be wrapped in the shroud of our self-confidence and buried in the tomb of our own ambitions. From this humble place, weakness arises into a boldness stripped of pride. Strength of ego transforms into powerful meekness in the Holy Spirit.

For many people called into vocational ministry, this is what the season of preparation is all about.

JOURNAL

Take a look at Philippians 3:4-10. List some of your greatest achievements and accomplishments that bring you the most satisfaction. Now consider them compared to "the surpassing greatness of knowing Christ Jesus." While these things make for a great resume, they can't compare to the treasure of divine relationship.

Called:
From a Power Position to a Humble Place

The angel of the LORD came and sat down under the oak in Ophrah that belonged to Joash the Abiezrite, where his son Gideon was threshing wheat in a winepress to keep it from the Midianites. When the angel of the LORD appeared to Gideon, he said,

"The LORD is with you, mighty warrior."

"Pardon me, my lord," Gideon replied, "but if the LORD is with us, why has all this happened to us? Where are all his wonders that our ancestors told us about when they said, 'Did not the LORD bring us up out of Egypt?' But now the LORD has abandoned us and given us into the hand of Midian." The LORD turned to him and said, "Go in the strength you have and save Israel out of Midian's hand. Am I not sending you?"

"Pardon me, my lord," Gideon replied, "but how can I save Israel? My clan is the weakest in Manasseh, and I am the least in my family."

The LORD answered, "I will be with you, and you will strike down all the Midianites, leaving none alive."

Gideon replied, "If now I have found favor in your eyes, give me a sign that it is really you talking to me. Please do not go away until I come back and bring my offering and set it before you."

And the LORD said, "I will wait until you return." JUDGES 6:11-18

"Threshing wheat in a winepress," translated, means "scared to death." God finds us regularly in places such as this. And rather than console, he calls. Of all the possible choices for a warrior, the Angel of the Lord chooses the most insecure coward. But note the Angel's stunning greeting, "The Lord is with you, mighty warrior."

I remember as a college student sitting in the balcony at church one Sunday morning. Rev. Wesley Putnam, a guest evangelist led the service. Upon discovering this, I slunk back in sluggish disengagement to wait it out. Rather than preaching, he enacted the story of Gideon. Something about Gideon's reluctance and insecurity resonated with me. More so, something about God's patient pursuit captured my heart. At the close, he sang a song with these lyrics:

> *God sees a lot in me.*
> *He sees someone no one else can see.*
> *He sees not what I am but who I can become.*
> *God sees a lot in me.*

A switch flipped deep inside my soul that morning. I emerged from my balcony hiding place with a strange confidence that these words were true. That was my secret yes to God's call. There would be several "fleecings" to come, but from that day I've never looked back.

So why this magnetic attraction to weakness, inadequacy and insecurity?

Something of the answer is in this exchange.

The LORD said to Gideon, "You have too many men. I cannot deliver Midian into their hands, or Israel would boast against me, 'My own strength has saved me.'" JUDGES 7:2

Why choose unqualified, ill-equipped and unlearned people? It's a cliché for sure, but it rings true: **"God doesn't call the qualified. He qualifies the called."** Take that to the bank. It's on every page.

But we have this treasure in jars of clay to show that this all-surpassing power is from God and not from us. 2 CORINTHIANS 4:7

JOURNAL

Take a few minutes and list all the things that seem to "disqualify" you from taking on a Divine assignment. List your liabilities—all the reasons why God should move on to someone else? What if this list is the "resume" God is looking for?

13 Called:
From One who Talks to One who Hears

The boy Samuel ministered before the LORD under Eli. In those days the word of the LORD was rare; there were not many visions. One night Eli, whose eyes were becoming so weak that he could barely see, was lying down in his usual place. The lamp of God had not yet gone out, and Samuel was lying down in the house of the LORD, where the ark of God was. Then the LORD called Samuel. Samuel answered, "Here I am." And he ran to Eli and said, "Here I am; you called me." But Eli said, "I did not call; go back and lie down." So he went and lay down. Again the LORD called, "Samuel!" And Samuel got up and went to Eli and said, "Here I am; you called me." "My son," Eli said, "I did not call; go back and lie down." Now Samuel did not yet know the LORD: The word of the LORD had not yet been revealed to him. A third time the LORD called, "Samuel!" And Samuel got up and went to Eli and said, "Here I am; you called me." Then Eli realized that the LORD was calling the boy. So Eli told Samuel, "Go and lie down, and if he calls you, say, 'Speak, LORD, for your servant is listening.'" So Samuel went and lay down in his place. The LORD came and stood there, calling as at the other times, "Samuel! Samuel!" Then Samuel said, "Speak, for your servant is listening." I SAMUEL 3:1-10

To some, the call of God comes early in life. Young Samuel postured himself to hear the voice of God. Picture this little boy, night after night, "lying down in the house of the Lord." Samuel lay right next to the most significant symbol in the history of the world—save the Cross, "the new Ark of the Covenant"—the vigilant presence of Almighty God next to a sleeping boy. Hannah named her son, Samuel, which means "God heard," because God heard her fervent prayer.

As Samuel grows in wisdom and stature and in the favor of the Lord, he becomes one who hears God. He needs help to understand. Thank God for Eli. I suspect Eli could have scolded the boy for interrupting his sleep. Instead he patiently paid attention. He helped the boy interpret the situation. Note he didn't instruct Samuel to stay up all night in prayer. He told him to "lie down" just as before. He coached Samuel in a way of readiness to respond instead of a striving urgency to entreat.

It comes down to seven words in the English language. Timeless and transcendent, these words capture the posture of one who would hear.

"Speak Lord, for your servant is listening."

These words do not initiate the conversation. They come in response to it. They don't come before God speaks. They come after.

God calls. We respond. God clarifies. We obey. We do not have to figure it out. God makes his word and will progressively plain to the heart postured to listen and obey. Maybe this voice came to you as a child and there was no Eli to guide you. Good news: That calling word of long ago still lives. It is never too late to respond, "Speak Lord, for your servant is listening."

JOURNAL

How do you "hear" the voice of God? Recount those times when that voice seemed plain and clear to you. Take a few minutes to encode this petition into your praying vocabulary. "Speak Lord, for your servant is listening." Often we over-dramatize the kind of experience we might associate with hearing the voice of God. What if it's more simple than we think? Ask the Spirit to "sanctify" your imagination. As you pray this prayer, be still and listen for inner impressions. Trust what comes. Write it down. Live with it over time. Sometimes a more relaxed approach opens us to hearing what all our straining deafened us to before.

 Called:
From Outward Appearances to Inner Person

The LORD said, "Take a heifer with you and say, 'I have come to sacrifice to the LORD.' Invite Jesse to the sacrifice, and I will show you what to do. You are to anoint for me the one I indicate." Samuel did what the LORD said. When he arrived at Bethlehem, the elders of the town trembled when they met him. They asked, "Do you come in peace?" Samuel replied, "Yes, in peace; I have come to sacrifice to the LORD. Consecrate yourselves and come to the sacrifice with me." Then he consecrated Jesse and his sons and invited them to the sacrifice.

When they arrived, Samuel saw Eliab and thought, "Surely the LORD's anointed stands here before the LORD." But the LORD said to Samuel, "Do not consider his appearance or his height, for I have rejected him. The LORD does not look at the things people look at. People look at the outward appearance, but the LORD looks at the heart." Then Jesse called Abinadab and had him pass in front of Samuel. But Samuel said, "The LORD has not chosen this one either." Jesse then had Shammah pass by, but Samuel said, "Nor has the LORD chosen this one." Jesse had seven of his sons pass before Samuel, but Samuel said to him, "The LORD has not chosen these." So he asked Jesse, "Are these all the sons you have?"

"There is still the youngest," Jesse answered. "He is tending the sheep." Samuel said, "Send for him; we will not sit down until he arrives." So he sent for him and had him brought in. He was glowing with health and had a fine appearance and handsome features.

Then the LORD said, "Rise and anoint him; this is the one."

So Samuel took the horn of oil and anointed him in the presence of his brothers, and from that day on the Spirit of the LORD came powerfully upon David. Samuel then went to Ramah. 1 SAMUEL 16:2B-13

The theme continues to develop. God chooses the unlikely to do the impossible. This time God chooses a man whose own father didn't consider him a candidate. The text bears repeating, "People look at the outward appearance, but the Lord looks at the heart." We spend enormous energy on outward appearances, but outward image does not matter to God. God searches for the inner image.

Isaiah, prophesying about the Messiah to come, said this,

He had no beauty or majesty to attract us to him, nothing in his appearance that we should desire him. ISAIAH 53:2B

The Apostle Paul says a similar thing in his letter to the Corinthian Church.

But God chose the foolish things of the world to shame the wise; God chose the weak things of the world to shame the strong. God chose the lowly things of this world and the despised things—and the things that are not—to nullify the things that are, so that no one may boast before him. 1 CORINTHIANS 1:27-29

If you feel unqualified to answer the call of God you are in good company. In fact, this may be your greatest credential. As a way of responding to the calling of God, offer up your weakness as a gift to God. Renounce trust in any worldly credential or accomplishment. What will it take for you to glory in your weaknesses? Consider that in your journaling. Now listen to Paul on the same point:

And so it was with me, brothers and sisters. When I came to you, I did not come with eloquence or human wisdom as I proclaimed to you the testimony about God. For I resolved to know nothing while I was with you except Jesus Christ and him crucified. I came to you in weakness with great fear and trembling. My message and my preaching were

not with wise and persuasive words, but with a demonstration of the Spirit's power, so that your faith might not rest on human wisdom, but on God's power. I CORINTHIANS 2:1-5

God is not so interested in human giftedness but in holy heartedness.

For the eyes of the LORD range throughout the earth to strengthen those whose hearts are fully committed to him. II CHRONICLES 16:9

JOURNAL

As an exercise in exploring calling, invite the Spirit of God to look upon your heart. Ask him what he sees. No one knew this more than David, the author of so many of the Psalms. Try praying this prayer from the Psalms and journal what comes in response.

Search me, God, and know my heart; test me and know my anxious thoughts. See if there is any offensive way in me, and lead me in the way everlasting. PSALM 139:24-25

15 Called: From Disillusionment to Insight

In the year that King Uzziah died, I saw the Lord, high and exalted, seated on a throne; and the train of his robe filled the temple. Above him were seraphim, each with six wings: With two wings they covered their faces, with two they covered their feet, and with two they were flying. And they were calling to one another:

> "Holy, holy, holy is the LORD Almighty;
> the whole earth is full of his glory."

At the sound of their voices the doorposts and thresholds shook and the temple was filled with smoke.

"Woe to me!" I cried. "I am ruined! For I am a man of unclean lips, and I live among a people of unclean lips, and my eyes have seen the King, the LORD Almighty." Then one of the seraphim flew to me with a live coal in his hand, which he had taken with tongs from the altar. With it he touched my mouth and said, "See, this has touched your lips; your guilt is taken away and your sin atoned for."

Then I heard the voice of the Lord saying, "Whom shall I send? And who will go for us?"

And I said, "Here am I. Send me!" ISAIAH 6:1-8

It seems Isaiah may have come to his calling by way of disillusionment. It took the death of the king Isaiah hoped in to bring him face to face with the King of all hope. In this way, disillusionment is a great gift. To become disconnected from one's illusions about life and reality opens the way to perceive the truth.

In essence, disillusionment is blindness. It is to look without seeing. The world can generate some pretty convincing illusions: wealth, power, prestige and fame, to name a few. The worldview and value system of the culture around us conspires to create a vision of the so-called good life. This vision first seduces. Then it blinds. In these scenarios, the call of God sounds like an alarm, awakening us to the shallows of our ambitions. Sometimes it takes losing a job or the death of someone near us. Despite great successes or tragic losses, God grabs our attention, opens our eyes and interrupts our best laid plans with an unforeseen intervention.

Isaiah saw the Lord. Then he saw himself. Then he saw the Light. Finally, he heard the call. Some scholars contend the meaning of the Hebrew language here suggests Isaiah "overheard" the voice of the Lord, as though God perpetually speaks these words. Isaiah had been listening but not hearing. Upon seeing and hearing Isaiah boldly responds, "Here am I. Send me!"

The irony comes when God sends him to a people who hear but do not understand and who see but do not perceive (See Isaiah 6:10). **Here's the kicker. Isaiah said yes to the call before he got the assignment.** May it be so with us.

JOURNAL

How do you identify with Isaiah's calling? Are your prior plans in the process Divine interruption? Can you hear the voice calling out, "Whom shall I send? And who will go for us?" Dare you utter those five bold words: "Here am I. S me!" The prophet would later write the words printed below. Begin a proces memorizing this text. It's one of the very core ideas we find in Scripture. It w serve you well as you pursue God's calling.

"For my thoughts are not your thoughts,
 neither are your ways my ways,"
 declares the LORD.
"As the heavens are higher than the earth,
 so are my ways higher than your ways
 and my thoughts than your thoughts.
As the rain and the snow
 come down from heaven,
and do not return to it
 without watering the earth
and making it bud and flourish,
 so that it yields seed for the sower and bread for the eater,
so is my word that goes out from my mouth:
 It will not return to me empty,
but will accomplish what I desire
 and achieve the purpose for which I sent it. ISAIAH 55:8-11

16 Called:
From "I can't do it," to "There's a fire in my bones"

The word of the LORD came to me, saying, "Before I formed you in the womb I knew you, before you were born I set you apart; I appointed you as a prophet to the nations."

"Alas, Sovereign LORD," I said, "I do not know how to speak; I am too young."

But the LORD said to me, "Do not say, 'I am too young.' You must go to everyone I send you to and say whatever I command you. Do not be afraid of them, for I am with you and will rescue you," declares the LORD.

Then the LORD reached out his hand and touched my mouth and said to me, "I have put my words in your mouth. See, today I appoint you over nations and kingdoms to uproot and tear down, to destroy and overthrow, to build and to plant." JEREMIAH 1:4-10

Talk about "dirty jobs." None can top the prophet Jeremiah. Some sense the calling of God on their life from their earliest days. God called Jeremiah in the womb. Despite this, most seem to find one way or another to disqualify themselves in the face of calling. Moses was too old. Jeremiah claims himself too young.

The reality of being called by God should be a normal occurrence among God's people. This does not imply that we should necessarily norm the particular ways God calls persons in Scripture. These stories instruct and guide us, though we need not insist on their experiences being replicated in our own. That said, many people through the centuries can point to a clear occurrence of calling in a defining encounter with the living God.

The God of the Universe, Father, Son and Holy Spirit, still speaks in particular ways to particular people. He still calls out to many listening ears, "Whom shall I send? And who will go for us?" On occasion he still whispers the names of those he calls in the watches of the night. Sometimes, the experience of a calling can be as dramatic as Jeremiah's. "I have put my words in your mouth." Wow! At other times, calling comes in the "still small voice" calling us forth from the caves of our fear.

All too often we actually run from the "called" life. One of the oft-cited poems of those who have struggled in responding to God is called, "The Hound of Heaven," by Francis Thompson. Here's an excerpt:

> *I fled Him, down the nights and down the days;*
> *I fled Him, down the arches of the years;*
> *I fled Him, down the labyrinthine ways*
> *Of my own mind; and in the midst of tears*
> *I hid from Him, and under running laughter.*
> *Up vistaed hopes I sped;*
> *And shot, precipitated,*
> *Adown Titanic glooms of chasmed fears,*
> *From those strong Feet that followed, followed after.*
> *But with unhurrying chase,*
> *And unperturbèd pace,*
> *Deliberate speed, majestic instancy,*
> *They beat—and a Voice beat*
> *More instant than the Feet—*
> *'All things betray thee, who betrayest Me'.*

Later in his prophetic writing, Jeremiah famously penned the futility of resisting the calling God placed on his life.

But if I say, "I will not mention him or speak any more in his name," his word is in my heart like a fire, a fire shut up in my bones. I am weary of holding it in; indeed, I cannot. JEREMIAH 20:9

JOURNAL

We all deal with internal and external resistance to the idea of pursuing the "called" life. Make two lists, one for internal resistance (i.e. fear I can't provide for my family, concern I'm not qualified or that my past disqualifies me) and one for external resistance (i.e. my family will disown me, my employer doesn't get it, etc.) Often, simply getting such things out of your mind and onto the paper can help your processing.

17) Called:
From a Static Job Description to a Series of Divine Assignments

The words of Nehemiah son of Hacaliah:

In the month of Kislev in the twentieth year, while I was in the citadel of Susa, Hanani, one of my brothers, came from Judah with some other men, and I questioned them about the Jewish remnant that survived the exile, and also about Jerusalem.

They said to me, "Those who survived the exile and are back in the province are in great trouble and disgrace. The wall of Jerusalem is broken down, and its gates have been burned with fire."

When I heard these things, I sat down and wept. For some days I mourned and fasted and prayed before the God of heaven. Then I said:

"O LORD, God of heaven, the great and awesome God, who keeps his covenant of love with those who love him and obey his commands, let your ear be attentive and your eyes open to hear the prayer your servant is praying before you day and night for your servants, the people of Israel. I confess the sins we Israelites, including myself and my father's house, have committed against you. We have acted very wickedly toward you. We have not obeyed the commands, decrees and laws you gave your servant Moses.

"Remember the instruction you gave your servant Moses, saying, 'If you are unfaithful, I will scatter you among the nations, but if you return to me and obey my commands, then even if your exiled people are at the farthest horizon, I will gather them from there and bring them to the place I have chosen as a dwelling for my Name.'

"They are your servants and your people, whom you redeemed by your great strength and your mighty hand. O Lord, let your ear be attentive to the prayer of this your servant and to the prayer of your servants who delight in revering your name. Give your servant success today by granting him favor in the presence of this man."

I was cupbearer to the king. NEHEMIAH 1:1-11

Jerusalem lies in ruins. Nehemiah, a faithful Israelite, lives in exile and serves as the cupbearer to the King of a foreign nation. The news reaches him about the devastation wreaked on Jerusalem: "The wall of Jerusalem is broken down, and its gates have been burned with fire." Note his response. He does not rise up in righteous indignation to go and do something about it. He sits down and weeps and mourns and fasts before God for several days.

It is tempting to look upon the ruins and devastation around the world and rise up with a spirit of resolve to go and do something about it—to go and take back the culture, to go and rebuild the nation. Need does not necessarily imply calling. Human need abounds. Our task lies in embracing the suffering and brokenness in the world around us deep in our hearts and from there presenting them to God in intercession. From Nehemiah's posture of prayer, comes a Divine assignment.

We can get so caught up in the pursuit of some worthy cause that we miss God's call. Divine assignments require a fluidity of heart. The Spirit of God cultivates in human beings a heart simultaneously bonded to the Father and broken for his people. This comes to us through a relationship of union with the Son. Jesus both demonstrates and develops in us a heart and mind after his own. From this place, we can receive any assignment God wants to give us. **This redefines calling as a series of vocational assignments rather than fulfilling a static "role" or "job description."**

As Nehemiah worked to fulfill the calling to serve as cup-bearer to the King, God brought him another assignment. As recounted in the next chapter, this place of service in the King's court funded the possibility for Nehemiah to fulfill the assignment to return to Jerusalem.

Father, show me your providence in my past labors. By your Wisdom, interpret my present vocation. Thank you for never wasting a day of my life. Bring all of my experiences into the service of your will. And by your shepherding Spirit, lead me in the way I should go. In the name of your son, our Lord, Jesus Christ, Amen.

JOURNAL

Look back over your life and think of the various seasons and stations from the perspective of Divine assignments. How can you interpret prior vocational pursuits from that angle? Were you at work on a Divine assignment unknowingly? Is there a particular assignment in your life at the present moment? A season of preparation itself must be understood in this framework. It's not a retreat from an assignment of ministry, but entry into a new assignment.

18 Called:
From a hopeless situation to hopeful preparation

After these things, during the reign of Artaxerxes king of Persia, Ezra son of Seraiah, the son of Azariah, the son of Hilkiah, the son of Shallum, the son of Zadok, the son of Ahitub, the son of Amariah, the son of Azariah, the son of Meraioth, the son of Zerahiah, the son of Uzzi, the son of Bukki, the son of Abishua, the son of Phinehas, the son of Eleazar, the son of Aaron the chief priest— this Ezra came up from Babylon. He was a teacher well versed in the Law of Moses, which the LORD, the God of Israel, had given. The king had granted him everything he asked, for the hand of the LORD his God was on him. Some of the Israelites, including priests, Levites, musicians, gatekeepers and temple servants, also came up to Jerusalem in the seventh year of King Artaxerxes.

Ezra arrived in Jerusalem in the fifth month of the seventh year of the king. He had begun his journey from Babylon on the first day of the first month, and he arrived in Jerusalem on the first day of the fifth month, for the gracious hand of his God was on him. For Ezra had devoted himself to the study and observance of the Law of the LORD, and to teaching its decrees and laws in Israel. EZRA 7:1-10

The favor of God tends to follow the prepared. It is said that Abraham Lincoln remarked in response to another of his early election failures, "I will get ready. My time will come." This must have been something of Ezra's mentality. Ezra lived as a prophet in exile. Despite discouragement and despair he persevered. He lived in a song-less generation among those who sat by the river and wept over Zion.

In the face of this, Ezra prepared. He studied the Law of Moses to the point of being "well versed."

"For Ezra had devoted himself to the study and observance of the Law of the Lord, and to teaching its decrees and laws in Israel."

Year after year, he prepared himself. And "the gracious hand of his God was upon him." This favor came not because of his faithfulness or in response to his devotion. The favor of God is the simple reality that follows in the wake of his Word. To dwell deeply in the Word of God is to live in the World of God's favor, despite any external circumstance. Human devotion does not cause Divine action. This is the essence of a "prosperity gospel." Human devotion merely knocks on the door leading to the realm of Divine activity.

"The King had granted him everything he asked." This is the favor of God.

Perhaps the larger issue at play here is not so much devotion as obedience. What if preparation for serving the will of God is a matter of devotion wrapped in obedience? **The will of God cannot be reduced to an outcome. It is a living way. Preparation cannot be reduced to a "preliminary" process. Properly conceived of, as preparation is ministry.**

Some consider a season of preparation a series of obstacles to navigate and hoops to jump through. They want to get to what they consider the "real" work. The wise see a season of preparation as a journey deeper into ministry rather than a retreat from it. Preparation might mean a few years of formal education. Other times, preparation may take the form of 20 years in exile. The key isn't so much about location as about preparation. Keep in mind, John the Baptist prepared 30 years for a six month ministry. Jesus prepared 30 years for a three year mission.

It behooves us to consider a few years of preparation for what may be a 30 or 40 year ministry. Don't you think? Somewhere along the way, someone asked Billy Graham what he would do if he learned he only had three years left to live. He wryly responded, "I would spend two of them preparing."

JOURNAL

What might a season of intensive preparation look like for you? Would it be formal or informal? What would you like to study more deeply? From whom would you like to learn in the history of the Church? How might you declare and enter into a "season of preparation" in your life right now?

19. Called: From Ordinary Faithfulness to Extravagant Obedience

"How will this be," Mary asked the angel, "since I am a virgin?"

The angel answered, "The Holy Spirit will come upon you, and the power of the Most High will overshadow you. So the holy one to be born will be called the Son of God. Even Elizabeth your relative is going to have a child in her old age, and she who was said to be barren is in her sixth month. For nothing is impossible with God."

"I am the Lord's servant," Mary answered. "May it be to me as you have said." Then the angel left her. LUKE 1:34-38

In all of Scripture and history, no calling rivals the calling of Mary. The Spirit of God, however, reveals through Mary the response befitting every calling. Another translation renders her words this way,

"Behold, the bondslave of the Lord; may it be done to me according to your word."

Like the Son she would bear, she takes on the nature of a "bondslave." She demonstrates a profound orientation to the reality of "Lordship." Mary shows us what pre-emptive obedience looks like. Her response captures the unconditional "yes," to the whatever, whoever, whenever, however, why-ever of the will of God. The "yes" of response precedes the call. **Mary's words do not represent the response of a "moment," but the "yes" of a lifetime.** Her words to the Angel merely confirmed the deepest reality of her soul.

How do we know the deepest reality of her soul? In the process of answering the call of God, she gave the Church a song. It opens with these profound lyrics,

"My soul magnifies the Lord, and my spirit rejoices in God my Savior."

Now is the time to learn this saying and sing this song. "Here am I, the bondslave of the Lord; let it be with me according to your Word. My soul magnifies the Lord, and my spirit rejoices in God my Savior." In these lyrics we find the true vernacular of the soul.

JOURNAL

This may seem rudimentary, but give it a try. Go back to the beginning of this journal and write these phrases on the footer of every page. Write the first one on the left page and the second on the right page. Do it in a spirit of simple worship. Write them until you can write them by heart. When you are done with that, try singing them. Over time, these practices will do something marvelous in your spirit.

20 Called:
From the Scripted Life to the Stories that Matter

By faith Abraham, when called to go to a place he would later receive as his inheritance, obeyed and went, even though he did not know where he was going. By faith he made his home in the promised land like a stranger in a foreign country; he lived in tents, as did Isaac and Jacob, who were heirs with him of the same promise. For he was looking forward to the city with foundations, whose architect and builder is God. HEBREWS 11:8-10

All these people were still living by faith when they died. They did not receive the things promised; they only saw them and welcomed them from a distance. And they admitted that they were aliens and strangers on earth. People who say such things show that they are looking for a country of their own. If they had been thinking of the country they had left, they would have had opportunity to return. Instead, they were longing for a better country—a heavenly one. Therefore God is not ashamed to be called their God, for he has prepared a city for them. HEBREWS 11:13-16

A powerful conversation occurs near the end of the epic, story-made-movie, *The Lord of the Rings: The Two Towers*. The unlikely heroic Hobbits, Frodo and Sam, find themselves discouraged to the point of despair. Their lives seem stuck somewhere in the long middle of the great story. Frodo is ready to throw in the towel. Sam reaches deep and speaks these inspired words to his friend:

> *It's like in the great stories Mr. Frodo. The ones that really mattered. Full of darkness and danger they were. And sometimes you didn't want to know the end … because how could the end be happy? How could the world go back to the way it was… when so much bad happened? But in the end, it's only a passing thing… this shadow… Even darkness must pass. A new day will come. And when*

> *the sun shines it will shine out the clearer. Those were the stories that stayed with you… that meant something. Even if you were too small to understand why. But I think, Mr. Frodo, I do understand. I know now. Folk in those stories… had lots of chances of turning back, only they didn't. They kept going… because they were holding on to something.*

Faith is not a proper belief, but a passionate grip. Yet faith calls for a release of control, a confidence in what can't be seen, an assuredness surrounded by doubt and discouragement, that determines to persevere anyway.

In the end, I think there is only one secret to following the Call of God. It's perseverance. Every enemy of God comes against the "Called" ones in an allied attempt to derail the story. The world, the flesh and the devil conspire to seduce, corrupt and destroy the fledgling plant of faith. **But every ounce of Heaven, the Father, the Son, the Holy Spirit, the Scripture and the Saints stand with all who want to respond to the calling of God.** Despite hardship, suffering and the constant threat of defeat, the battle between Heaven and Hell is the mismatch of the ages. "He who is in you," says John, "is greater than He who is in the World" (1 John 4:4).

The posture of the Called is humble kneeling. The prayer of the Called is, "Come Holy Spirit!" The battle cry of the Called is, "Thy Kingdom Come!"

The perseverance of the Called is not one of "bucking up" or "trying harder" or "optimistic self talk." The biblical idea of perseverance is distinct. It requires a steadfastness, yet underneath this is a hyper-focus. It comes together in statements like, "For he was looking forward to the city with foundations, whose architect and builder is God," and "They did not receive the things promised. They only saw them and welcomed them from a distance" (Hebrews 11:10, 13).

The writer captures this dynamic kind of focus as he sums up the storytelling at the beginning of the next chapter. The great secret is not to focus on them but on Him. Let us behold them beholding Him, and as our beholding shifts to Him, our lives will become like them.

Therefore, since we are surrounded by such a great cloud of witnesses, let us throw off everything that hinders and the sin that so easily entangles, and let us run with perseverance the race marked out for us. Let us fix our eyes on Jesus, the author and perfecter of our faith, who for the joy set before him endured the cross, scorning its shame, and sat down at the right hand of the throne of God. Consider him who endured such opposition from sinful men, so that you will not grow weary and lose heart. HEBREWS 12:1-3

What would it mean for us to fix our eyes on Jesus? What will it take to get our gaze off of ourselves? What would a life look like that was completely and astonishingly abandoned to the beholding of this God? It is from Him we have come, and it is in Him that we live and move and have our being, and it is to Him we are going. The climax of the prayer found on the breastplate of Saint Patrick defines this persevering hyper-focus:

Christ with me, Christ before me, Christ behind me, Christ in me, Christ beneath me, Christ above me, Christ on my right, Christ on my left, Christ in breadth, Christ in length, Christ in height, Christ in the heart of every man who thinks of me, Christ in the mouth of every man who speaks of me, Christ in every eye that sees me, Christ in every ear that hears me.

May it be so with us.

JOURNAL

What hinders this kind of hyper-focused perseverance in your life? What sin easily entangles you? What scares you about pursuing the calling of God? What common elements do you find in the stories through Hebrews 11?

21 Called: To the Future of the Possible

But whatever was to my profit I now consider loss for the sake of Christ. What is more, I consider everything a loss compared to the surpassing greatness of knowing Christ Jesus my Lord, for whose sake I have lost all things. I consider them rubbish, that I may gain Christ and be found in him, not having a righteousness of my own that comes from the law, but that which is through faith in Christ—the righteousness that comes from God and is by faith. I want to know Christ and the power of his resurrection and the fellowship of sharing in his sufferings, becoming like him in his death, and so, somehow, to attain to the resurrection from the dead.

Not that I have already obtained all this, or have already been made perfect, but I press on to take hold of that for which Christ Jesus took hold of me. Brothers, I do not consider myself yet to have taken hold of it. But one thing I do: Forgetting what is behind and straining toward what is ahead, I press on toward the goal to win the prize for which God has called me heavenward in Christ Jesus. PHILIPPIANS 3:7-14

Nothing captures the call of God more than these words from Paul to the church at Philippi. The calling Paul continually articulates comes down to one all consuming ambition, "to know Christ."

He says to the Corinthians, "For I resolved to know nothing while I was with you except Jesus Christ and him crucified" (1 Corinthians 2:2).

He prays for the Ephesians, "That the God of our Lord Jesus Christ, the glorious Father, may give you the Spirit of wisdom and revelation, so that you may know him better" (Ephesians 1:17). "I pray that out of his glorious riches he may strengthen you with power through his Spirit in your inner being, so that Christ may dwell in your hearts through faith" (Ephesians 3:16-17a).

He clarifies his mission to the Colossians, "My purpose is that they may be encouraged in heart and united in love, so that they may have the full riches of complete understanding, in order that they may know the mystery of God, namely, Christ" (Colossians 2:2).

Seeing a theme? **Paul's calling finds its beginning, middle and end in one thing: Knowing Jesus.**

Paul says it most clearly from a dank prison cell when he writes, "I want to know Christ and the power of his resurrection and the fellowship of sharing in his sufferings, becoming like him in his death, and so, somehow, to attain to the resurrection from the dead" (Philippians 3:10-11).

Graham Kendrick, one of the best song writers of our time, put these lyrics to music and gave us a hymn for the ages (only time will tell). If you don't know the tune, find it. This is the song of the called.

All I once held dear, built my life upon
All this world reveres, and wars to own
All I once thought gain I have counted loss
Spent and worthless now, compared to this

Knowing you, Jesus
Knowing you, there is no greater thing
You're my all, you're the best
You're my joy, my righteousness
And I love you, Lord

Now my heart's desire is to know you more
To be found in you and known as yours
To possess by faith what I could not earn
All-surpassing gift of righteousness

Oh, to know the power of your risen life
And to know You in Your sufferings
To become like you in your death, my Lord
So with you to live and never die.

JOURNAL

Take a few minutes and slowly, deliberately copy the words to Philippians 3:10-11 (see previous page). Set a timer for 5-10 minutes and write the text over and over, with the devotion of a scribe. The aim isn't speed or count, but sheer love of the Word of God. Write it on your gate, put it on your doorpost, bind it to your wrist, write it on your forehead, talk about it with your children when you get up and lie down and when you walk along the road (my paraphrase of Deuteronomy 6).

You are the Called of God and this is your calling.

Epilogue

Therefore, I urge you, brothers and sisters, in view of God's mercy, to offer your bodies as a living sacrifice, holy and pleasing to God—this is your spiritual act of worship. Do not conform any longer to the pattern of this world, but be transformed by the renewing of your mind. Then you will be able to test and approve what God's will is—his good, pleasing and perfect will. ROMANS 12:1-2

What is the will of God for my life? That's the question I asked for so long and the one I am most often asked. According to the text above, the will of God means walking in the way of Jesus in the power of the Holy Spirit. To know the will of God is the outcome of becoming a particular kind of person and walking down a particular path. The plan unfolds as we offer our lives as a living sacrifice. The details start coming as we are converted from the patterns of self centered living to the mind of Christ.

To attempt to forecast the "will of God" for one's life is an exercise in futility. The God we follow doesn't offer a map or GPS device. He offers himself. Looking ahead one could never predict it. But when one looks back along the unlikely path travelled there is a deep sense of, "I wouldn't trade that journey for all the money in the world." No matter the specific vocation or destination, to walk in this way of abandoned trust always and inevitably leads to the beautiful life. This way of life, like the wine at the wedding feast in Cana, keeps getting better and better, transforming from good to pleasing to perfect.

Blessed are those whose strength is in you, whose hearts are set on pilgrimage… They go from strength to strength, till each appears before God in Zion. PSALM 84:5,7

Author's Note

Thank you for the encouragement you've given me by working through this little "field-guide" of sorts. I would be thrilled if we could continue the conversation at jdwalt.com. Please also visit the treasure trove we are calling "Seedbed," at asburyseedbed.com. Resources like this one and others will continue to spring up.

J.D. Walt is the Sower in Chief of Seedbed Publishing. He also serves as Vice President for Community Formation at Asbury Theological Seminary.

About Seedbed

Seedbed is sowing for a great awakening through publishing resources aimed at the whole Church. Visit **asburyseedbed.com** for our daily Feed and Store, featuring a range of print and digital media resources.

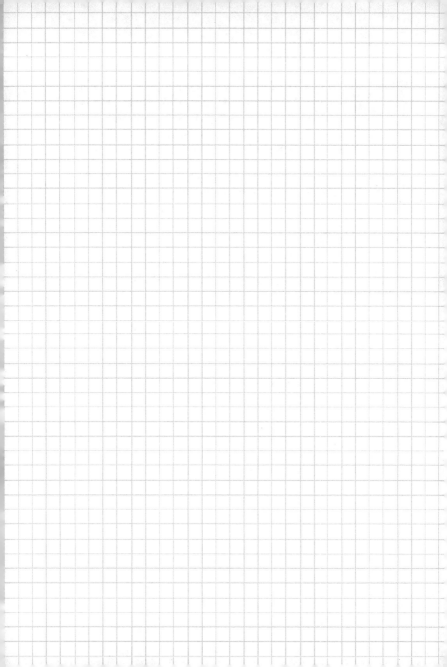